AF476923

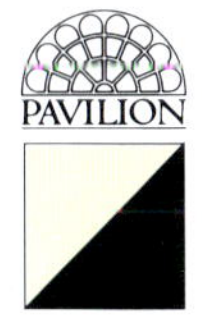

POCKET PAINTERS

BURNE-JONES

1833 — 1898

Burne-Jones

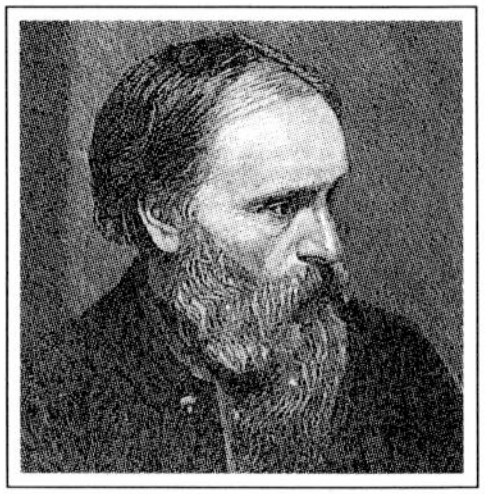

Edward Burne-Jones (1833-1898) was
born in Birmingham and had a
somewhat sad and solitary childhood.
His mother died a few days after his
birth, no other children having
survived, and he was brought up
largely by his bible-wielding nanny.
Thrown back on his own resources,
he lived within his own imaginative
world, feeding on tales from myth
and legend and drawing pictures of
what came into his head rather than
what was before him. If ever a child was

father to the man it was Edward Coley Burne Jones – the hyphen came later.

Sickly in appearance, he was nevertheless a high-spiritied child, and popular at school for his pranks and cartoons. In his teens he devoured Romantic poetry, then became deeply interested in religion and decided to aim for the Church. In 1852 he went up to Oxford, and there met William Morris with whom he shared a love of medievalism and a hatred of the industrial age. Recognizing in the work of D.G. Rossetti a kindred spirit and potential guide, they both had second thoughts about the Church and determined to meet their hero.

Rossetti was no disappointment, and helped them develop their talents. In London it was soon apparent that the young friends had different priorities: for Morris, the practical, if Quixotic, aim of using craftsmanship to combat the soullessness of the industrial world; for Burne-Jones, escape from its ugliness into a beautiful past, peopled by melancholy knights and pale, unattainable women.

Burne-Jones was largely self-taught as a painter, and he learned much of his art in the galleries of Italy. From the fifteenth-century masters he derived his predilection for gem-like colours and sumptuous decoration, and the Greek, Christian and Arthurian traditions provided the subject-matter for his idyllic fantasies. While few would deny that the tapestry and stained-glass window designs he produced for Morris & Co. are wholly successful, to some modern eyes. There is perhaps too much refinement and not enough life and realism in this dream world where, as Quentin Bell has said, *'everyone is quietly and decently sad.'* There was even a certain amount of ridicule at the time, notably from W.S. Gilbert in *Patience*. Nevertheless, Burne-Jones enjoyed considerable success. Indeed he was that rare phenomenon – a talented artist who was showered with honours in his own lifetime. Moreover, of the two distinct strands of 'Pre-Raphaelism', it was not the naturalism of Holman Hunt but the decorative medievalism of Burne-Jones which, by giving birth to the Aesthetic Movement and Art Nouveau, had the wider influence.

Burne-Jones never claimed to be facing reality – in fact he specifically denied it – but the sheer beauty of his alternative world is beyond dispute ◪

*The Legend of
St Frideswide*

Oil cartoon
1859
406 × 140 cm

How well Burne-Jones's art suited
stained-glass window design was
already evident in the richly coloured
St Frideswide window at Christ
Church Cathedral in Oxford, for which
this is one of the oil cartoons. His
designs were a vital source of income at
the beginning of his career, and his
main contribution to Morris's
company.

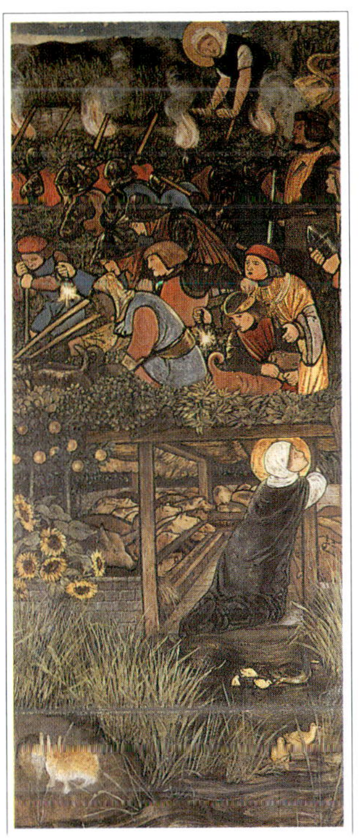

The Musicians
(detail)

Tempera
c.1860
25 cm diam.

When Morris moved into Red House
at Bexley Heath in 1860, his friends
helped with the furnishing and
decoration – a collaboration which led
to the foundation of the original
company. This is a detail from one of
seven tempera paintings planned for
the dining-room, of which only three
were completed.

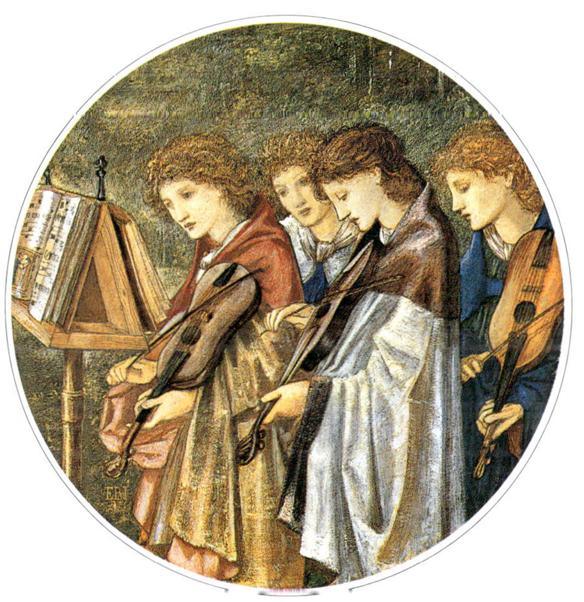

The Lament

Watercolour with
bodycolour
1866
47.5 × 79.5 cm

In the 1860s, like Albert Moore and,
briefly, Whistler, Burne-Jones turned
to classical sources. He studied the
sculptures at the British Museum,
notably the Elgin marbles, and here
produced what Ruskin had been
advocating: a composition of classical
tranquillity, in which narrative has been
expunged, and draughtsmanship
improved.

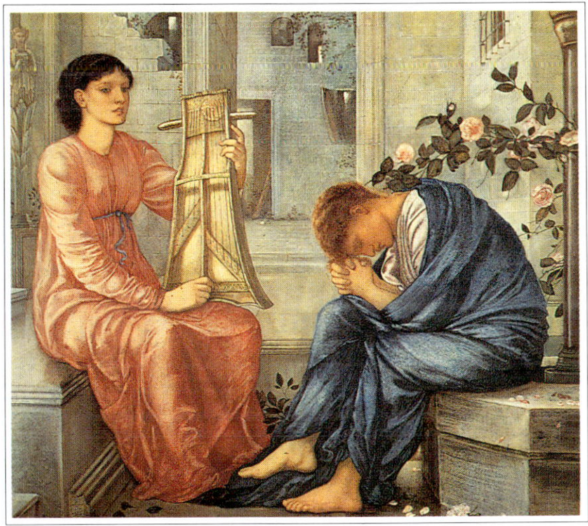

Green Summer

Oil on canvas
1868
65 × 106 cm

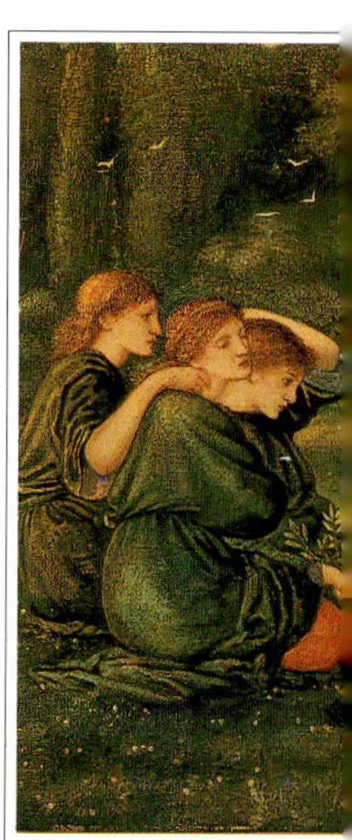

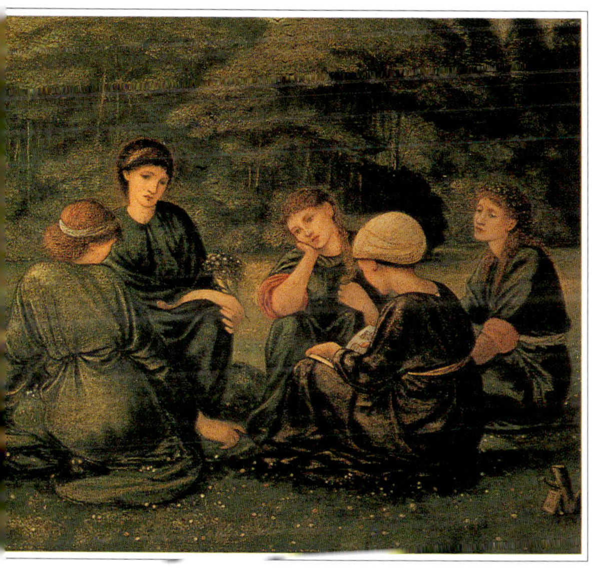

*St George
and the Dragon*

Gouache
1868
73 × 47 cm

This may hurt a little. The apparent
delicacy with which the knight applies
the sword, the complaisance of the
beast and the equanimity of the
hostage are typically unrealistic, but as
a decorative arrangement the picture
has a stunning effect.

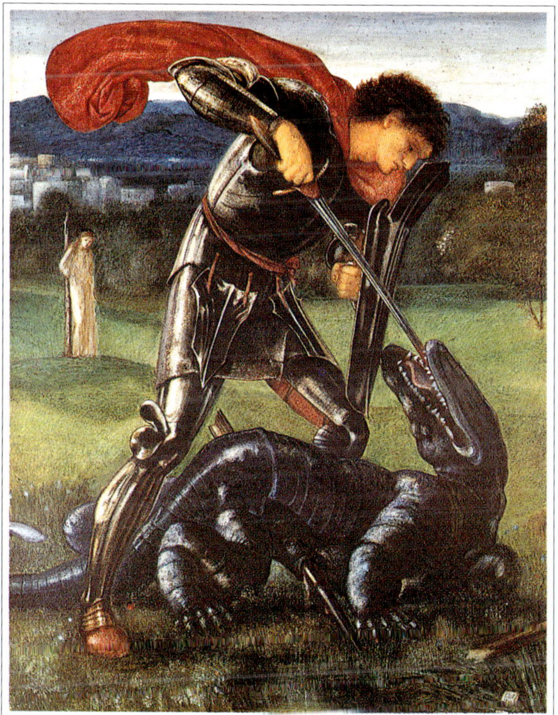

Summer

Gouache
1869
122.5 × 45 cm

In the *Seasons* series of gouaches commissioned by Frederick Leyland, the figure of *Summer* was modelled by Maria Zambaco, a Greek sculptress for whom Burne-Jones nursed feelings of exceptional tenderness; that of *Winter* by his wife Georgiana.

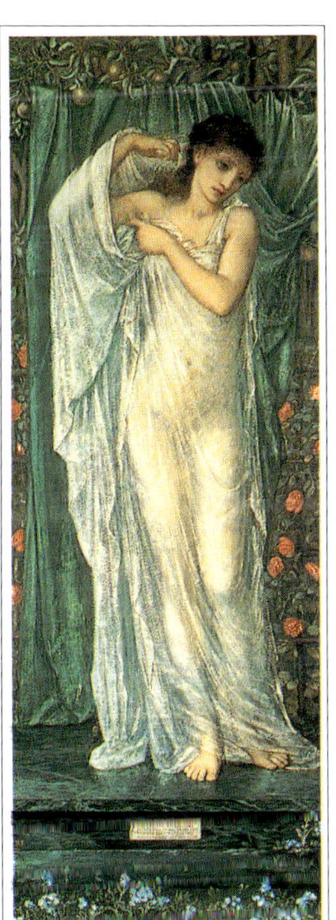

Winter

Gouache
1869
122.5 × 45 cm

The elongated format of the *Seasons* would have felt very familiar to Burne-Jones as a result of his stained-glass window designs. Meanwhile the icon-like figures were doubtless the kind of subject which gave his work such allure for the likes of Aubrey Beardsley.

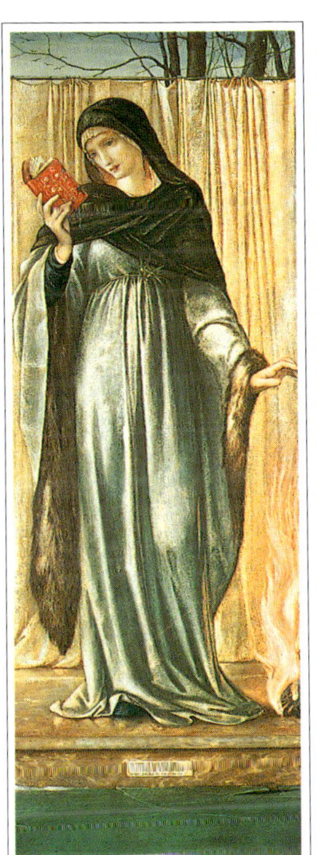

Laus Veneris

Oil and gold paint
on canvas
1869
122 × 183 cm

Maria Zambaco frequently posed for
Burne-Jones. Here she represents a
sensuous Venus lolling with her
maidens, for whose beauty five young
knights appear to be about to lose
their sanity. The painting refers to the
Tannhäuser legend, in which a knight
falls tragically under the spell of the
Enchantress.

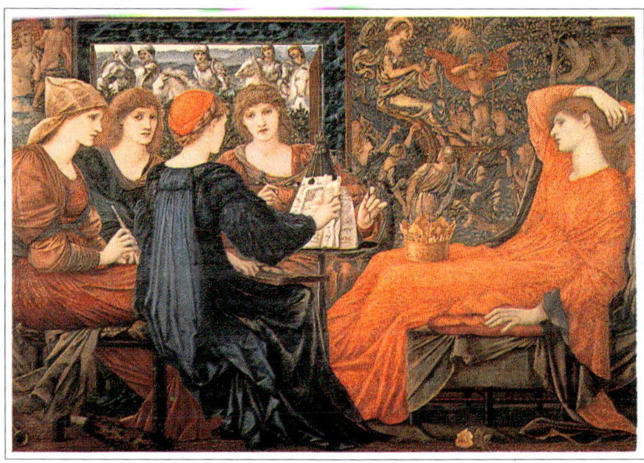

The March Marigold

Oil on canvas

c.1870

72 × 77.5 cm

The tranquil harmony of the landscape
and the monumental treatment of the
figure suggest a classical inspiration for
this sublimely delicate painting. One
suggestion is that it is based on the
legend of Psyche.

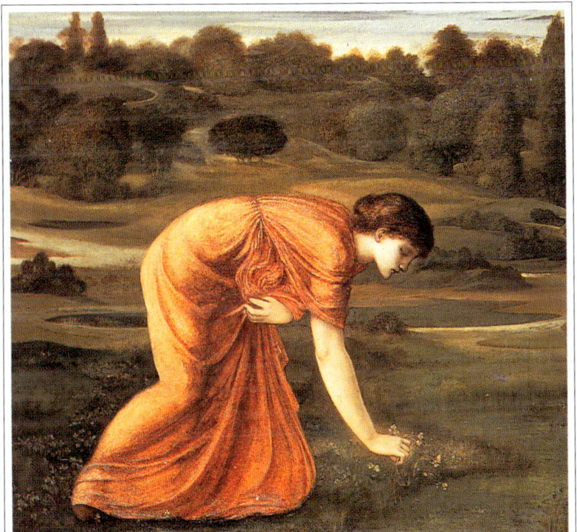

Temperantia

Watercolour
1872
152.5 × 58.5 cm

The much publicized opening in 1877 of the Grosvenor Gallery, at which Burne-Jones's depictions of Temperance, Hope and Faith were exhibited, gave his reputation a welcome boost. For the eleven years of its existence the gallery was in the vanguard of fashion, and Burne-Jones began to circulate as a Society painter.

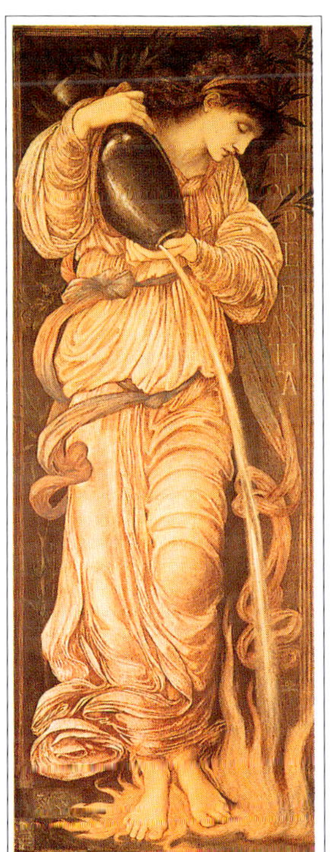

The Mirror of Venus

Oil on canvas

1870 – 76

120 × 200 cm

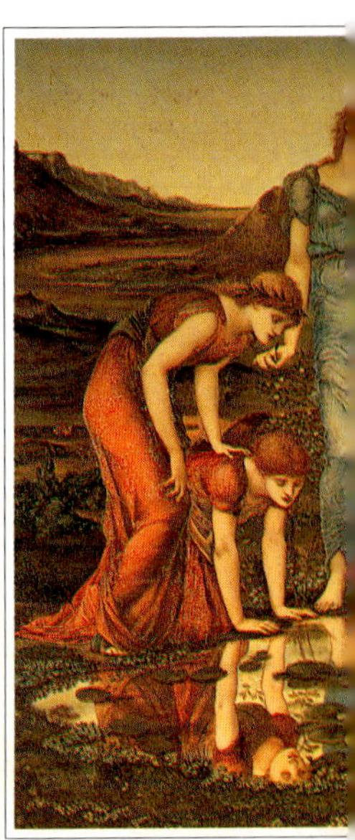

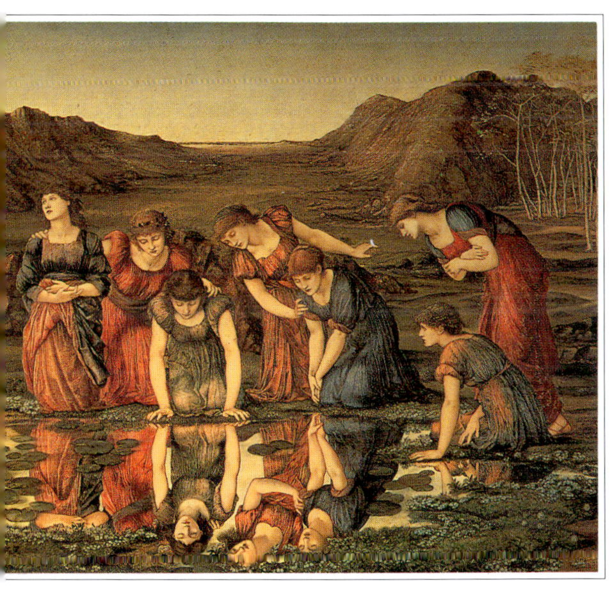

Previous page – This was also among the eight Burne-Jones works to be shown at the first Grosvenor Gallery exhibition. Here the paintings were hung to greater advantage than at the Royal Academy, on walls painted green and yellow. Hence W.S. Gilbert's famous jibe at the Aesthetes in *Patience:*
'A greenery-yallery, Grosvenor Gallery Foot-in-the-grave young man!'

The Hours

Oil on canvas
1870 – 82
86.5 × 183.5 cm

'I mean by a picture a beautiful romantic dream of something that never was, never will be – in a light better than any light that ever shone – in a land no one can define or remember, only desire.'
Edward Burne-Jones.

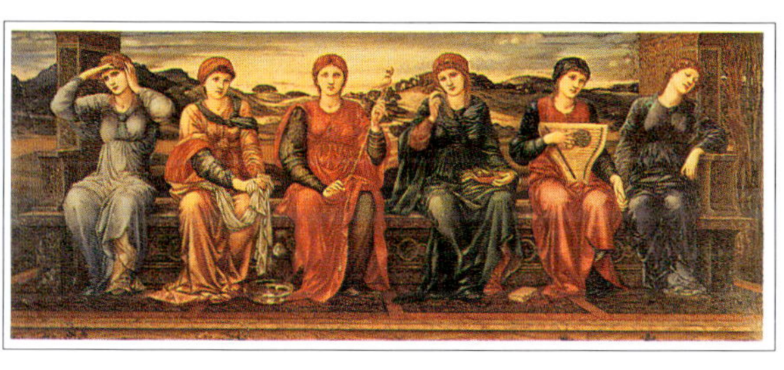

The Mirror of Venus

Gouache
c.1885
15 cm diam.

This delicate little gouache is one of a
series of his favourite themes, each
linked with the name of a flower, with
which Burne-Jones would amuse
himself when ill in bed. They were later
published in a limited edition under
the title of *The Flower Book*.

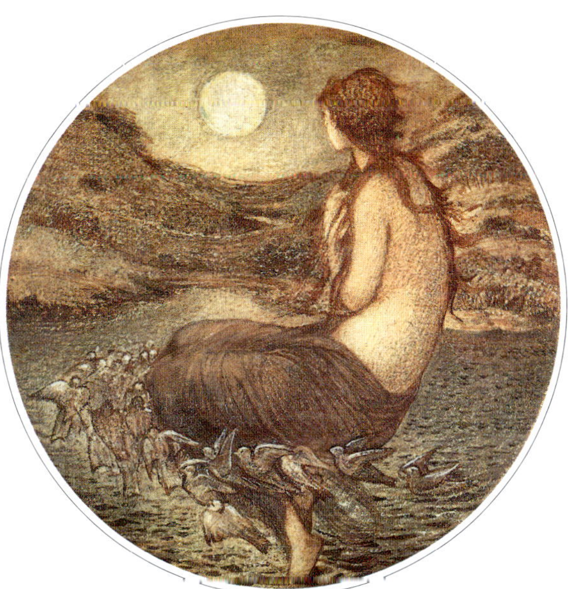

The Adoration of the Magi

Tapestry
1887 – 90
346 × 503 cm

Apart from the company's very first tapestry, which Walter Crane designed, Burne-Jones was responsible for all of Morris & Co's tapestry designs from 1881 until 1894. As time went on the compositions grew larger and more complex. This sumptuous design was followed by the even more ambitious *Morte d'Arthur* series.

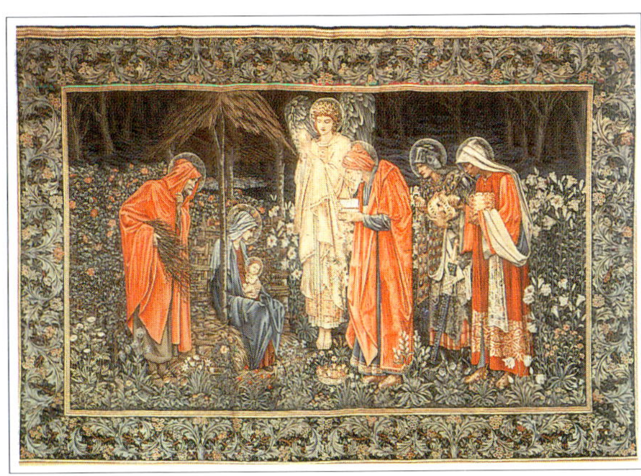

*The Legend of the
Briar Rose:
The Garden Court*

Oil on canvas
1870 – 90
122 × 238 cm

The Briar Rose series of paintings, based
on the story of *Sleeping Beauty,* was
commissioned by Alexander
Henderson, who later installed them at
Buscot Park, near Faringdon,
Oxfordshire where Burne-Jones added
connecting scenes, so that they formed
a continuous decorative frieze.

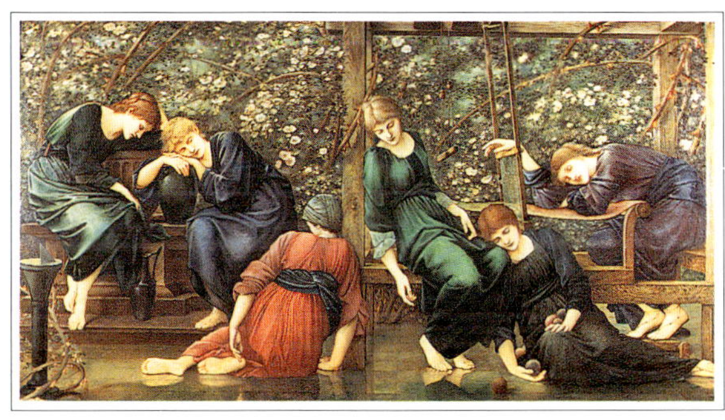

The Legend of the
Briar Rose:
The Sleeping Beauty

Oil on canvas
1870 – 90
122 × 229 cm

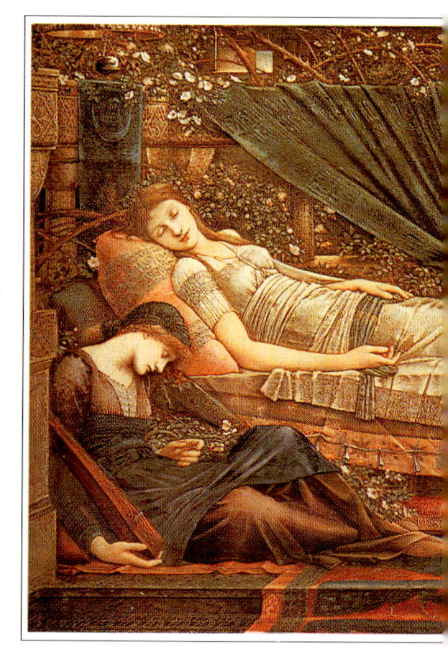

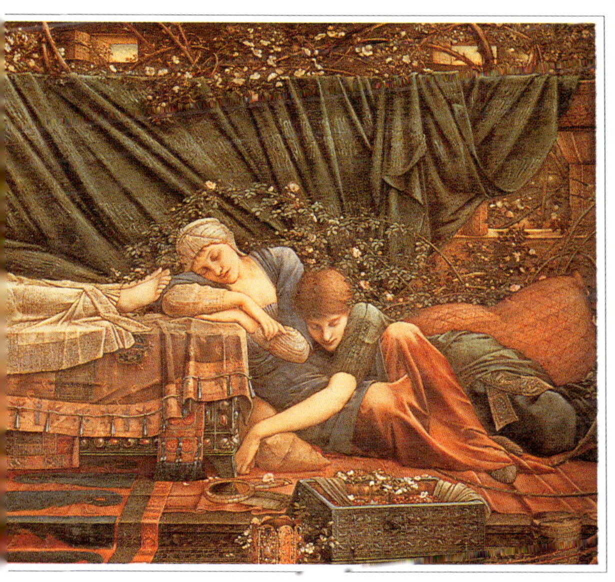

Angel

Oil on canvas
c.1890
95 × 75 cm

A distinction which gave Burne-Jones no satisfaction at all was his influence on the young Aubrey Beardsley, who disconcertingly declared himself to be his disciple. Burne-Jones regarded Beardsley's decadent style with abhorrence, as a perversion of his own pure and honest draughtsmanship.

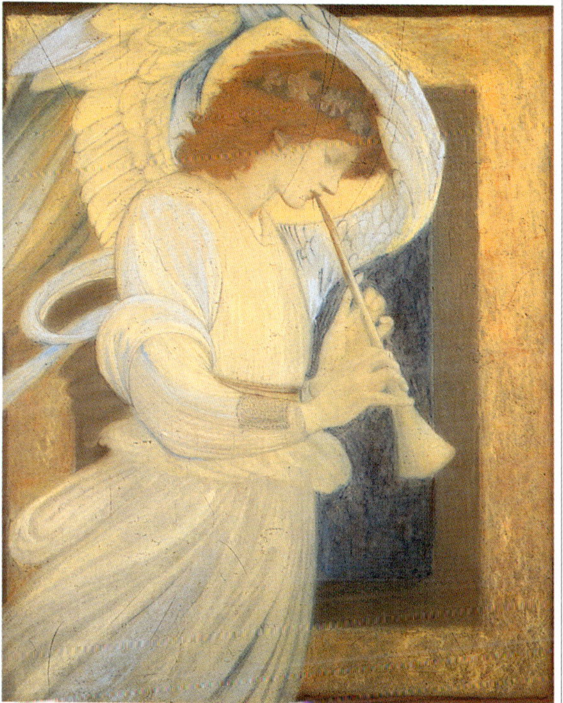

Music

Oil on canvas
c.1894
95 × 50 cm

'Only this is true, that beauty is very beautiful, and softens, and comforts, and inspires, and rouses, and lifts up, and never fails.' Edward Burne-Jones

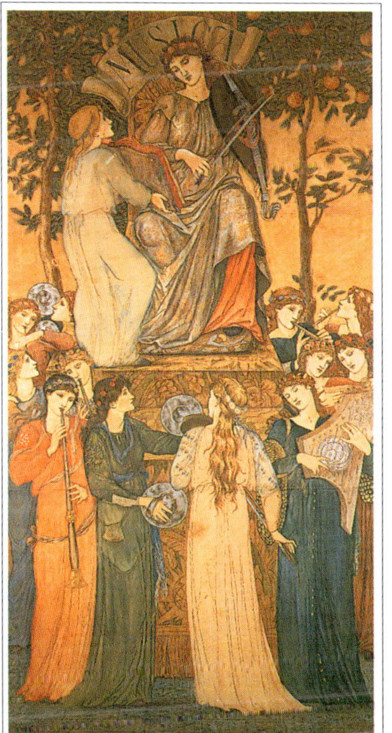

*The Pilgrim at
the Gate of Idleness*

Oil on canvas
1896 – 7
110 × 150 cm

Chaucer provided Burne-Jones with
numerous subjects. This is a scene from
his allegorical *Romaunt of the Rose,* itself
a translation of a thirteenth-century
French romance. Here Burne-Jones is
returning to a design he had originally
made for a tapestry.

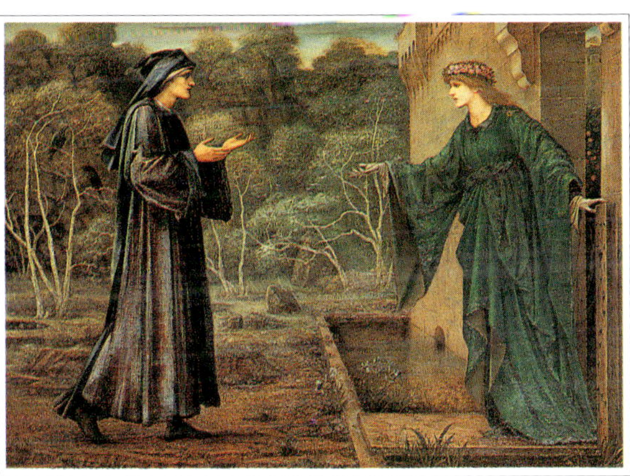

*The Sleep of
Arthur in Avalon*

Oil on canvas
1881 – 98
111 × 254 cm

Burne-Jones once said that the stories
he most liked to paint were those he
had enjoyed as a child. The legend of
King Arthur was one of them, and as
his own death drew near he found
himself identifying with the sleeping
king. He never completed the painting.

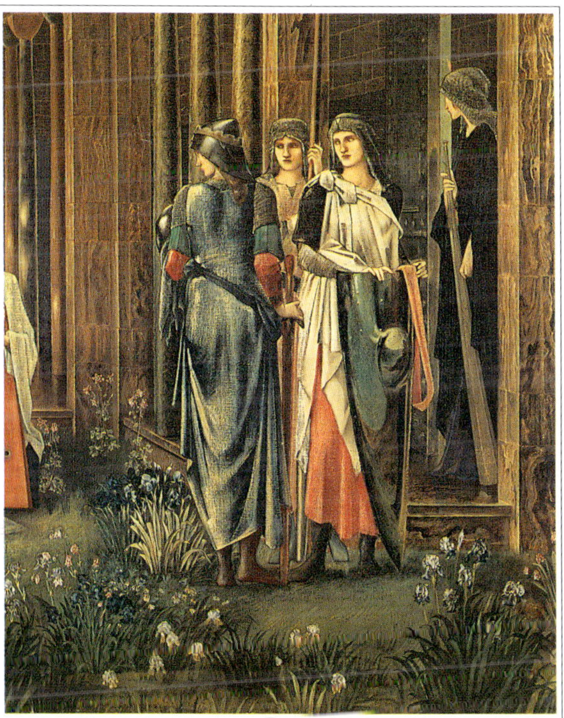

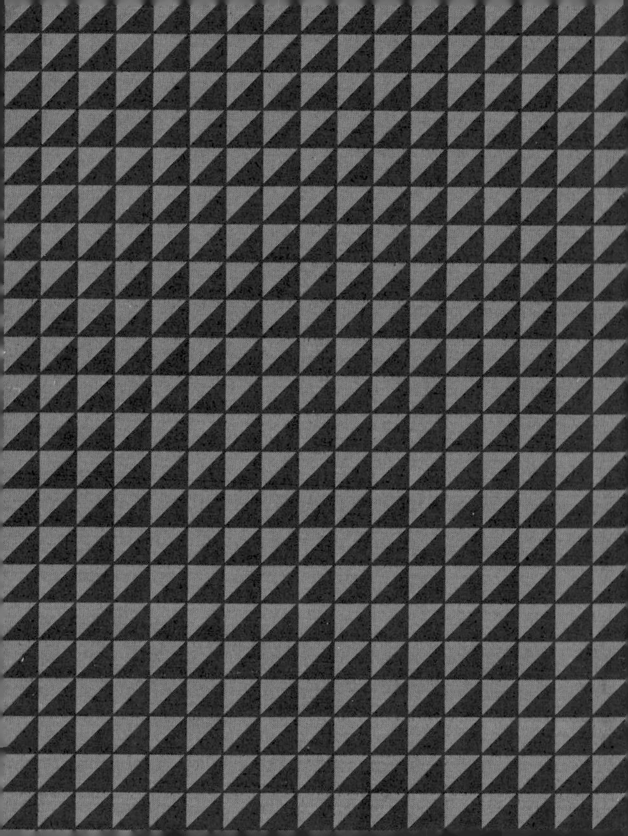